**FONDAZIONE
SANDRETTO RE REBAUDENGO
PER L'ARTE**

Dreams

edited by Francesco Bonami
and Hans Ulrich Obrist

This book has been realized on the occasion of the 48°
Esposizione Internazionale d'Arte – The Venice Biennial of
Visual Arts – to be free handed out during the press days
Venice 9-12 June 1999

Original Graphic Concept: Riccardo Gemma
Revised Graphic Concept: Claudia Colasanti and Maurizio Ceccato
Cover Photo: Armin Linke
Cover Design and Page Layout: Maurizio Ceccato
Editing and Revision of Proofs: Lisa Dasteel,
Claudia Colasanti and Barbara Papuzzi

CASTELVECCHI ARTE

c/o Castelvecchi Editoria & Comunicazione srl
Commissioning Editor: Claudia Colasanti
Editor: Laura Liotti
Via G. Severano 33 - Roma 00161
tel. 06/44252414 - 44252489
fax 06/44252438
ISBN: 88-8210-155-X

FONDAZIONE SANDRETTO RE REBAUDENGO PER L'ARTE

Corso Stati Uniti 39
10129 Torino • Italia
tel. 39 011 5625536
fax 39 011 549225
e-mail: write@fondsrr.org
web: www.fondsrr.org

Thanks to:
Armin Linke and all the other artists for having dreamed
with the Fondazione Sandretto Re Rebaudengo per l'Arte.

Sogni/Dreams

edited by Francesco Bonami
and Hans Ulrich Obrist

Sogni/Dreams – project of the Fondazione Sandretto
Re Rebaudengo per l'Arte – has been included as an
a latere event of the Venice Biennial of Visual Arts.

ASTELVECCHI ARTE

FONDAZIONE SANDRETTO RE REBAUDENGO PER L'ARTE

The Fondazione Sandretto Re Rebaudengo per l'Arte was established in Turin in 1995 with the aim of providing a focus for new generations of artists, critics and curators. It operates in the world of art in as wide-ranging a manner as possible to supply a showcase for research and the production of work by the most interesting and challenging artists today. Our goal is to enable an ever wider public to learn about the changes and trends in contemporary art.

The Fondazione extends its attention and energies on all visual arts from painting to sculpture, photography, video, installation and performances. It organises exhibitions, congresses, seminars, study activities, workshops for children, publications and prizes.

It has set up collaborations with other cultural centres both in Italy and abroad as well as with public and private institutions to create an open dialogue and cultural exchange.

In 1997 the Fondazione inaugurated a new space in Guarene d'Alba: Palazzo Re Rebaudengo, an 18th century building, has been transformed into an exhibition space for international contemporary art.

The Fondazione Sandretto Re Rebaudengo per l'Arte, since its establishment, has been particularly interested in being present at the Venice Biennial of Visual Arts. In 1995 the exhibition *Campo 95* was held at the Corderie dell'Arsenale in Venice on the occasion of the Biennial centenary; in 1997, during the XLVII Venice Biennial, the Fondazione exhibited at the Venice cinema Accademia the project *Loco-Motion, Contemporary Art on the Border of Cinema.* This year the Fondazione also wanted to be present and this book – an *a latere* event of the Venice Biennial – is its contribution to this year's 48° Esposizione Internazionale d'Arte.

EDITORS' NOTE

Dear.........................,

It is very often the case that real ideas transmute into unrealizable dreams. We look back and forth swinging between nostalgia and science-fiction, only rarely we think about our dreams as a necessary possibility for our present.
Sogni/Dreams is a project that wants to dream about realizable and unrealizable dreams and make them real and possible.

Years ago Patrizia Sandretto Re Rebaudengo dreamed about a place where contemporary art could find fertile grounds, where ideas could become reality. She created first a Foundation, the Fondazione Sandretto Re Rebaudengo per l'Arte, a symbolic space where art is happening in different places. Today her dream has become a reality, a site where projects, dreams and ideas will converge into one space. In the near future Patrizia Sandretto Re Rebaudengo will inaugurate a new building in Torino where the Foundation will operate and will present the reality of contemporary art dreams. The space designed by the Architect Claudio Silvestrin will be one of the few buildings for contemporary art in Italy built from scratch. Moreover, the building will not be an isolated reality, an ivory tower. The new space will appear in a central area in Torino and will share its grounds with the grass roots reality of the city.

Sogni/Dreams wants to celebrate the Foundation's new building but it also wants to celebrate the possibility of ideas expanding and being spread into the world simply but effectively.

We chose Venice because it contains, more than any other city, the reality of dreams. It is a city that wants to survive transforming the past into a proposition for the future, nostalgia into necessity, time into activity.

We have selected more than 100 visual artists to share with us one of their necessary dreams, ideas they would like to see become a reality while still alive to enjoy it.

Once all the dreams are collected, we will publish 50.000 copies of a small book to be distributed during the next Venice Biennial.

We would be very happy if you will accept our invitation to be one of the selected artists and will send us one of your dreams in a format no longer than 300 words.

Your participation is very important to us and we are looking forward to hearing from you soon. Our deadline is April 30th.

Thank you and Best Regards,

Francesco Bonami
Hans Ulrich Obrist

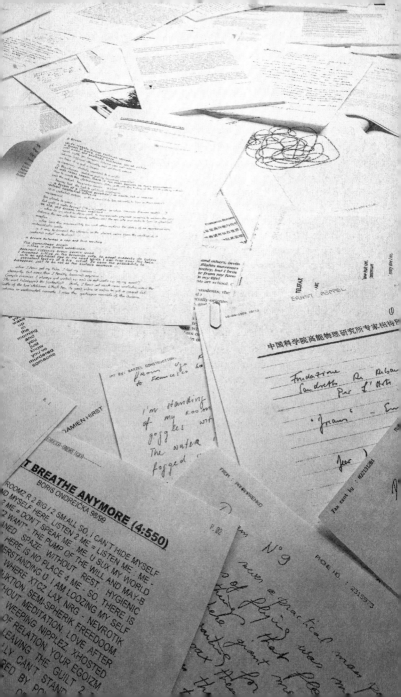

MARTINE ABALLÉA MARINA ABRAMOVIĆ DOUG
AITKEN LAYLAH ALI PAWEL ALTHAMER ARAKI
GASTON BACHELARD MIROSLAW BALKA
OLADÉLÉ BAMGBOYÉ MATTHEW BARNEY
MASSIMO BARTOLINI BECK SIMONE BERTI JOHN
BOCK CHRISTIAN BOLTANSKI LOUISE BOURGEOIS
MATHIEU BRIAND MAURIZIO CATTELAN WILLIAM
J. CLANCEY GU DEXIN HERI DONO JIMMIE
DURHAM MARIA EICHHORN OLAFUR ELIASSON
JAN FABRE HANS–PETER FELDMANN TERESITA
FERNÁNDEZ ARIS FIORETOS URS FISCHER ALICIA
FRAMIS KATHARINA FRITSCH GIUSEPPE
GABELLONE ALBERTO GARUTTI ANNA GASKELL
DR. GATEV GILBERT & GEORGE LIAM GILLICK
DOUGLAS GORDON JOSEPH GRIGELY JOHAN
GRIMONPREZ CAI GUO-QIANG CM VON
HAUSSWOLFF THOMAS HIRSCHHORN DAMIEN
HIRST CHRISTINE UND IRENE HOHENBÜCHLER
CARSTEN HÖLLER RONI HORN HUANG YONG
PING FABRICE HYBERT TAKASHI IKEGAMI ANN
VERONICA JANSSENS ISAAC JULIEN ILYA &
EMILIA KABAKOV WILLIAM KENTRIDGE KOO
JEONG-A LUISA LAMBRI JOHN LATHAM
TEODOLINDA VON LIBITSCH ARMIN LINKE
KEN LUM CHRISTINA MACKIE MASAMI
AKITA PAUL McCARTHY STEVE McQUEEN JONAS
MEKAS ANNETTE MESSAGER BORIS ONDREIČKA
GABRIEL OROZCO PANAMARENKO JENNIFER
PASTOR MANFRED PERNICE RAYMOND PETTIBON
MICHELANGELO PISTOLETTO PAOLA PIVI ERNST
PÖPPEL EMILIO PRINI CHARLES RAY JASON
RHOADES PIPILOTTI RIST UGO RONDINONE
ISRAEL ROSENFIELD BOJAN SARCEVIC THOMAS
SCHÜTTE JIM SHAW YINKA SHONIBARE
ANDREAS SLOMINSKI YUTAKA SONE RUDOLF
STINGEL SABURO TESHIGAWARA EINAR
THORSTEINN WOLFGANG TILLMANS RIRKRIT
TIRAVANIJA ROSEMARIE TROCKEL TUNGA LUC
TUYMANS FRANCISCO J. VARELA RICHARD
WENTWORTH GILLIAN WEARING FRANZ WEST
IAN WILSON CORNEL WINDLIN WONG HOY
CHEONG CERITH WYN EVANS CHEN ZHEN

I

There are vampires with different coloured blood: some have red blood, others have orange or blue blood. They wear silk kimonos the same colour as their blood. There is a green vampire of which I am particularly fond. I stay close to him. I am walking along a road and a yellow vampire starts chasing me. But I run away and he not catch me.

All these vampires are members of a secret society. Right now they are meeting on the upper floor of a wooden building which looks like a bathing pavillion. The ceiling is very high. The walls are covered with inscriptions and drawings which are incomprehensible. I am rather sceptical about the beliefs of this society. The meeting is attended by a lot of old women. I look for the green-blooded vampire, but I cannot see him anywhere.

I leave. I find myself in a park. I see a Japanese man meditating. I ask him if he has seen a man in a green kimono. With a wave of his hand, he shows me some trees where several of them are sitting in the branches.

II

There is a small stone house in the countryside that is almost in ruins, overgrown with plants. When you approach it, or when you talk about it, you automatically speak in rhyme.

Extract from Martine Aballéa, «Prisonière du sommeil» edited by Michel Nuridsany, published by Flammarion.

Martine Aballéa

I dreamt that my brother Velimir was buying a nuclear bunker in Amsterdam from some Armenian.
The bunker is built from red bricks and has many entrances.
The bunker is deep underground.

Marina Abramovic

Doug Aitken

i dream of a mountain with no summit.

I went to sleep with my camera to photograph my dream. And I did. Then I awoke from that dream.

Nobuyoshi Araki

RIGHT AND WRONG DREAMS

Not the right kind of dream

Dream (3/3/99): On a bus with Bill Clinton. Bus encounters road construction and has to stop. They are building a special bridge for the bus to take so we will have to wait. Then the bus moves but doesn't take the special bridge, going instead to the right (bridge is built flat on top of highway). Did the shooting start then or before the bus lurched forward? State troopers pull out black guns and fire into the windshield. My seat companion and I hurl to the floor; I recall that being flat on the ground is best in such a situation.

Right kind of dream 1865

Freedom from eternal servitude

Right kind of dream 1963

All children... black, white... Jews, Gentiles... go to school – no, sit at table... together

Right kind of dream 1999

We don't need that much, here have some, please... take more

That which precedes all dreams

The Top 20 Percent of the population wandering around the world – a great shopping spree – there is art everywhere.

Laylah Ali

The people are pampered, multicultural; they like spicy food and airy rooms, white-walled. On the perimeter, there are angry people. They are eating too many carbohydrates (that is one popular theory); even complicated sugars feed their anger. They cough too much and complain in their separate newspapers about the air quality downwind.

Meanwhile, the 20 Percenters have never felt better. They live, on average, for 123 years and have much more time to think and travel. They believe that all the angry people want is to be like them – they are sure of this – and point to various contented members who were recent descendants of «complainers».

When I was ten

It was of revenge; a knife plunged in the backs of class-mates; white people – all of them – realizing what a TERRIBLE mistake they had made; money coming mysteriously in the mail; the timely intervention of strangers; escaping from the fire that was certain to engulf our home.

My lifetime

Same as above but translate differently, not so literal-ly. Read acts of violence as «bloodless upheaval». Take «white» off people. Interpret «money by mail» as «enlightened democratic socialism». See again «that which precedes all dreams».

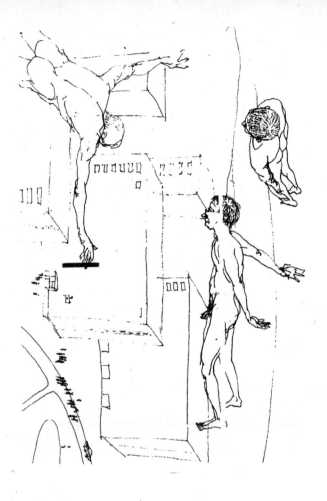

I dreamt about a friend who came to see me wearing a Diesel jacket and said, «I bought this jacket because they said it helps you fly. But I can't even get off the ground. Why don't you have a go?» «Gladly». I put the jacket on and soared above the church spires. I remember the thrill of ascent. At the same time, I knew that the capacity of flight depended on a subtle belief in levitation. Whenever my belief faltered, I clearly began to lose altitude. Shortly afterwards, I had a dream about flying over a park.

As the promenading crowd looked on, I gained momentum and took off, seeing their startled faces. I spread my arms, happy as a bird in the knowledge that I could fly. I soared above the treetops. I had my first dream about flying when I was about seven. During a birthday party, I started levitating above my bed until I felt the ceiling against my back. The guests smacked their lips in admiration. I know I really would fly if only I had faith. I could take to the air from the top of the Palace of Culture in Warsaw; I could walk on water. But my faith is weak. Its weakness is due to a nagging rationalism. For all its usefulness, rationalism undermines the «idiotic» assurance that one can fly, converse with the dead, and have out-of-body experiences. Most people yearn for a world without gravity. Take American slang, where «fly» has practically become a synonym of «cool»; take TV commercials: women's hair in shampoo ads is no longer material, while the people in the GSM mobile phone spots travel without touching the ground. The laws of physics no longer seem to apply to cosmetics and mineral water. Take sports. Isn't ski jumping a form of levitation? Take fast driving. They're all symptoms of a nostalgia for the ethereal, reminiscences of a former state when we had no bodies and could soar freely, cover any distance. When we were pure free will. My project for a figure hovering above the earth concerns urban space. The concept can be traced back to Antiquity when monumental architectural forms and statues first distinguished and adorned important parts of cities. As figurative sculpture has always been most common, I would like to use 20th century technology (a helium-filled structure) in order to «sculpt» a monumental human figure and suspend it over part of the city undergoing rapid development. I am interested in relating the «antique» or ancient motive of colossal sculpture to huge construction projects like the Pyramids, temples or monuments. There is also the interesting connection between a rational city and an irrational idea: a «sculpture» in the air, a dreamlike situation. A place which is already extraordinary by virtue of the accumulation of modern architecture being built all at once, is now a place where the unexplained happens: the appearance of a human-shaped balloon «watching» the city from an aerial perspective. Yet another odd tourist attraction, a funny touch in a dignified setting, perhaps. For one of the sightseers-tourists has been elevated.

be in good company now and later

At the end of the 18th Century the priest Baka said: «This is the place where we will spend most of our lives».
He meant the cemetery.
Cemeteries are beautiful and powerful traces of human beings, although they contain a lot of chaos. The neighborhoods of people in graveyards are random in most cases.
My project is to break this tradition in such an important place as a cemetery.
In life we meet different people. Some of them become our friends. The moment of death separates us.
Although our bodies earlier were intimate acquaintances, they become separated and are put in different holes in different places all over the world.
But we can be close together forever in the neighborhood of friends, during life and after death.
My project is to establish the building of a cemetery for friends. For the friends I already know and those that I hope to meet in life.
The place should be chosen together by all of us.
The form too.
The list of people should be open

Miroslaw Balka

I dream of singing Sandii's «Dream Catcher» to Taeko.

Oladélé Bamgboyé

A reoccurring dream setting:
This setting reoccurred in dreams between 1972 and 1973. I was five years old. Each dream was set in the kitchen of the house where I lived in Mill Valley, California. Cabinets hung on the wall above the kitchen counter top.

Under the cabinet where a paper towel dispenser would typically hang, there was a 2 ft. by 1 ft. by 1 ft. wad of crumpled up aluminum foil. Occasionally the wad of foil would open up, unraveling onto the floor. From inside the foil, a middle-aged woman would emerge who helped my parents with various jobs around the house. She was a sympathetic character, liked by my family, although she frightened me. I would wake up from the dream whenever the woman would look at me directly in the eyes.

I would like to see a sequoia growing in the middle of a European city. A large square occupied initially by a shoot, then by a young tree and finally by this vegetable skyscraper. Care for the tree would be entrusted to a family that would pass down the task from generation to generation.

Massimo Bartolini

MASAI TICKET FOR AL

Ticket for the outpost shoutghost
Zoot suit trashwelder
Parachute revelator
Root digger
Bird thrower
Janitor vandal

Passage of bug ticket
For the matchstick traveller
Chaos beautician
With crankcase earwax
Greaselight thumbtacks
Half a moustache like a pirate broom

Hep-ho Al
Smokestack Al
Paper bag Al
Colorblind Al
Voodoo Al
My rocking horse guillotine
My backseat rhyme-master

«Pull down your pants and do the hot dog dance»

Shot pistol jazzes up their asses
My man Al revolving door spitting out holy debris
Dismantler of cankerous machinery

Fertilizer of barren lanes
Resurrector of phantom skins
Redeemer of disposables
Litter bug of escape hatches and back doors
Orchestrator of the moment movement.

One breathable intercourse
Constructor of invitations to the garbage life
The garbage moonlight
The garbage love

Digging on Al
Here's the letter I meant to send
Here's the bent ticket and no more rent
Here's to you and your thing Al
Always Al
And always Al
And love to Al

Sometimes, dreams can present structures of association that concern the dreamer's interests. In some cases, my dreams take the form of a script or at least have a narrative development.

MONOMANIA

22/02/1997, night: a boy of medium height and a cartoonlike expression, thin, slightly hunched and with a sad nose and pale eyes wanders here and there. The setting is not fixed as normally happens in dreams (our character could come out of a Texas saloon and find himself next to a Swiss motorway or a fishing village by the shores of a Norwegian fjord). Having said this, let us move on to the central part of the story: the curious characteristic of our protagonist and the sole justification for his existence. Every time someone sat or made a movement suggesting that he intended to sit or lean against a wall, etc., our boy ran towards him, took up a position behind him and acted as a backrest, in such a way that the person about to sit could use him in that way. The situations he preferred were those in which there was a stool with no backrest. This boy had no family; no one knew who his parents were or what his name was, but everyone knew him as the «backrest boy».

PHOBIA

10/01/1998, night: the doctor, with a slightly diffident expression, observed the man opposite him. He could not understand whether the latter was being sincere or not, and he felt slightly as if he were being fooled. In his studies and in his experience as a psychoanalyst, he had never come across a case of... how to define it? This man was not scared of open spaces, nor did he have problems of claustrophobia but, or so he said, he felt uncomfortable in normal spaces: in those of average size.

Simone Berti

Meech's feverish action, the preliminary phase of schizophrenia, is in the terminal phase. The unstable matter and cerebral matter restrict amateurs, the Mopedhoney and peasant farmers of the high arid grounds and the silo crops.

The farmer floats iodine through the umbilicus of the calves' stomachs. Straw all around Meech's bucket – Meech's riverbed.

2000 litres of bovine jet scribble over his macro-world enclosed by an electric fence. Farmland consolidation against the conductive friction of the peasant girl's love. Lombard rate and discount rate dissolve expanded polystyrene with patex.

The cooper's «Bolwieser» is emulated by his servant. The recipient is changed into an economic man by art welfare. The recipient's arm stretches out to model artistic thoughts. Almost-I-myself-me touches the micro-existence-game of the incompetent inter- preter's life. One million soft toys wait inside–outside in me-mind. The mutant flattens out and flees from the OP polystyrene under Ah oui Ah non.

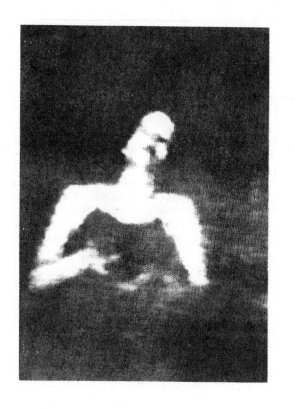

Christian Boltanski

Last night I dreamed that I was on the phone with Carol Rama:

You must be Francesco Bonami listen what I dreamed «I saw the gate and the wall and the wall was not straight but with many corners and I kept walking along the wall and by the time I got to the end of it was dark or maybe it was dark just around the last corner».

The Dream of the Superstition Contradicted is a Nightmare

Louise Bourgeois

How could I penetrate dreams when reality lives inside me?

I believe that this a reasonable wish.

The Holy Grail of particle physics is a simple theory in which all the forces, albeit different in appearance, are joined in nature to form a single force. The latest data collected using the electron-positron collider suggest that this is what might happen if a new idea, super-symmetry, proves correct.

I am delighted by the thought that schizophrenia and conscience might be coupled, because I hope that the bastard elaborated by a controlled environment would no longer be an insidious disease.

It might be the point of collision, the product of all vices. By doubling reality, we might perhaps be struck by the utmost uncertainty; it might surprise us during our quiet sleep.

But it would be even worse to trigger it off, to master its flight from existence, the frequency of its appearance, to make it symmetric to life. As it developed, it would become a real virus of thought, a champion of intrusion and a genius of evasion; it would be brief, rapid, precise, instantaneous, robbing reality, the time to create a temporary autonomous mental space, as a good terrorist, the founding father of a mental rhizome and as a good citizen, the henchman of the conscience.

It is an idea that makes me wish that my prick were real. I dream of frightening myself.

Dear Vittorio
did YOU receive the invitation to SOGNI/DREAMS?
Kisses
Valerio

Of course!
do you have any to lend me?
ciao
m

Dear Vittorio
the trouble is that I never dream
because I never sleep
kisses
Valerio

William J. Clancey

Mars, a place to go

Creatures of habit, looking only at our feet, we too rarely see the planets and moons of outer space as a place, somewhere to go. In your town you see a new park, and there you may walk. In a book, you read of a city, and see on the map where you may travel. But twenty years ago men walked on the moon. Have you looked at their travel pictures? Have you seen the mountains and dusty hills? When you look up and see the moon, do you imagine it as a place where you can go? Have you seen the valleys of the moon?

Now further off is Mars, too far to see directly as a land. But already we travel to Mars with cameras and robots. We circle Mars with satellites and look down on huge ancient volcanoes. We are starting to know Mars as a place where we can go. Imagine being there, a desolate place, with desert beauty. Perhaps soon we shall send a plane or a balloon to fly through the long, yawning valleys. On your television, you will see Mars as easily as the American southwest desert. Will you begin to see Mars as a place to go?

Before a long journey, comes a dream of travel, a thought of being somewhere, of seeing and feeling its nature. As our robots move like toys on Mars, we see already where we shall walk, what cavernous rilles we will explore, the plains on which we will build new towns. Now we design habitats and greenhouses, tomorrow, colonies. Melting the ice cap, we might sow life and create air to breathe. We are walking already in the rusty land of Mars, on our neighboring planet, dreaming of a place to go.

I hope that the project will be sponsored in one area in the world, no matter where, and be realized in another part of our globe.

First of all, we would photograph each sponsor and add one of his phrases to each picture.

Transferring this material to the site of the project we would choose a suitable area for its realization.

For example, in Turin center we would select

–a lawn to be «covered with fruits»

–a street to be «covered with candies»

–a square in which «a two tier platform would be built. The upper tier to be laid with butter and jam, the lower to be laid with bread»

–a space in which «a huge transparent container full of fruit wine» would be placed.

–a building on which «dolls will be hung»

–a wall where «the sponsors pictures with their slogans would be hung»

The project will be carried out at night.

In 1963 Vivian Ayers, D Minor, and others, invited me to join an arts group for the beginnings of the Civil Rights movement in the U.S. South. It was mostly a group for theater and poetry, but I brought into it an 'uneducated' visual art practice that came from my family traditions. That was such a free and purposeful time in my life!

I have long wanted to make an anti-art school. (The *anti* refers to the school, not art).

There would not be teachers and students; there would be colleagues. (All colleagues would be paid).

The agenda would be based on socially-oriented intellectual investigations, away from text, narrative, and language. Based on that part of human intellect that is not language nor metaphor for a linguistic construct. Based at the same time on the idea of discourse with the most intelligent «person-on-the-street»; that is, trying to engage intelligence without having made a judgement about where it might be found. (Such as, for example, academia, or one social class or another).

In this anti-school we would not train ourselves, nor pursue skill nor strategy.

Any or all of us might at any given moment *make* some object; using whatever material or technique. (Such as photos, re-placing or mis-placing things, assembling things, even painting). The anti-school would provide needed materials without having a permanent set-up of pre-existing materials.

Colleagues would not necessarily, maybe not even usually, come from within the art community, and the anti-school's agenda would not be primarily to function within the art community.

In 1970, along with Roque Carmona, Danielle Fiard, and Gonzalo Torres, I tried to begin such a *center* in Geneva, but that city was too poorly rich to support such an effort.

In the mid 1980's I moved to Mexico with the specific idea of starting such a *center*. Our collegial group consisted of Carmen, a prostitute who wanted a bit more from life, and five street kids, Carlos, Jose, Juan, Miguel Angel and Santiago.

Because of rough politics and rougher social and economic realities we could not maintain; nor keep our hearts from breaking.

Still, or probably more now, I hold this dream.

Jimmie Durham

Who discovered Dreams? Everybody has dreams, sometimes familiar sometimes strange.

Dreams exist in real life when people are awake. Many people have experiences in which they come to a place they remember they had already been before, but in a dream which happened a long long time ago –déjà vu! Because there are a lot of illusions and superficial and artificial lives in this material world, we often do not look at reality through our heart's eye.

Indonesia is an island – country with more than 13,000 islands. There are a lot of artists living in the country and many of them live in the forests. They do their work everyday, day and night, for offerings in their religious ceremonies. An artist working in this system is like a mediator between a community, religion and priest/shaman. They communicate through oral culture, texts, dance, shadow-play, symbolism in textiles, and ritual offerings, etc. They also use sound, facial expressions, metaphors which they never put into verbal form but are understandable to themselves.

In Java people learn about the meaning of their dreams through a holy book called «Primbon». Adepts of this book give knowledge to the people concerning the naming of children, the correct site of their houses, the location of rice fields, etc, using the constellation contained in the book as a guide.

Heri Dono

Dreams give knowledge of people who are sensitive or aware of these metaphysical phenomena. These phenomena cannot be understood merely through words because they have different paradigmas from conventional symbols. They become a guide for our present life and our future as well as for our past through an agreement between human beings.

The world looks like a blooming flower in a process of growing up, passing away, and returning as a reincarnation, immortality.

The idea of a millenium is not universal because different cultures have their own different calendar systems. In Bali, for instance, in one year there are two New Years, as well as only 5 days in a week.

Nowadays we still live in a material world. I think it would be much better to share our artistic and cultural inspirations with different kinds of people. In today's perspective we no longer believe in the distance between the self and the other, because everyone and everything have become subject matter. This idea is more clearly represented by the Mandala (the wheel of life) in which all of us are standing in the middle of it, in one world.

I dream that thousands of gods and angels are flying everywhere in our world. They are giving energy, hope, and inspiration to human beings as well as happiness and spiritual fulfilment.

Olafur Eliasson

I have twice dreamt that I died. The first time was about 2 years ago. I was driving in the countryside in Iceland with my father, his wife, my sister and my friend Gunner and I think also his daughter. It was sunny and cool weather when we saw a small abandoned stone house with a terrace going around it. For no particular reason we were walking around the house and behind the house I noticed that the shiny knee-high grass was growing from the familiar Icelandic black wet sand. I had a thin walking stick in my hand when I noticed that the sand was moving as if I were standing on a buried waterbed. Being worried for my friends and family I shouted to them to watch out for quick sand. The next moment I was stuck in the sand to my waist, trying to use the pathetic thin stick to stop sinking. Shouting at the others I quickly sank to my neck and just as I saw them arriving and shouting at me, the muddy sand closed on my face. The sand was wet and cold but in particular I remember the pressure of the sand on my body. The cold pressure of the sand quickly strangulated my whole body and I died. Just like that. No particular sense of being dead arrived. I felt nothing, just simply nothing.

The second time I died was not long after the first, though the setting was a bit different.
I was sitting high on a mountain side over a horse-shoe shaped fjord. It must have been evening since the light seemed to be moonlight. The fjord was covered with ice which in the light was glowing nicely. High from my position up on the mountain I, without wondering, saw myself at the foot of the mountain walking out on the ice as if I wanted to cross it. The ice seemed strong and after walking a few steps on it, it totally disappeared. Only a small piece was left with me sitting on it.

Now the water was totally dark, and obviously I was thinking that some large fishy monster was about to reach the little ice flake floating around in the middle of the fjord with me on it. Since I was only experiencing this from the mountain side, too far away to shout, I could only guess at my state of mind. Soon the piece of ice started to float around as if something was pushing it from underneath, and the next moment the ice flake was mowing rapidly in circular patterns making it very difficult for me to stay on the ice. Finally I fell into the water, and the ice disappeared as well. From the mountain side I was shocked, and as the minutes passed without me resurfacing, I realised that I was dead. I felt an empty sadness and guilt as I walked down the mountain.

A few times I dreamt that I crashed with an airplane – actually I dreamt this twice while flying – but I always woke up just before the plane hit solid ground, thus avoiding the experience of impact. I am always relieved about this last minute wakeup, as this way I avoid questioning my strong belief that if I indeed do crash, I will survive somehow. This belief is what keeps my fear of flying from totally controlling my traveling.

I dread the third time that I'll dream my life ends – for some reason the third time seems crucial – the fourth or fifth can never be as bad as the third. Recently I spoke to Patricia, who is doing this book, and she cheered me up with her Italian belief that dreaming about your death prolongs your life by 10 years (each time), which in this case means that I will at least live to be 51.

Maria Eichhorn

I have a dream

A performance – a sculpture?

I'm walking for 7 days and 7 nights and making a kind of ball (a globe?) two times the size of myself. The ball I make so carefully is made from the materials of the surface I'm walking on.

When I think the ball of «provisions» is ready it must be moved to a right and suitable place. Then a new journey begins. I push the ball with my feet and walk with my hands, moving backwards with my head down.

I push this load behind me by alternate thrusts to the left and the right.

One would expect that I choose a smooth road on at least a gentile incline. Not at all!

I'm looking for a steep slope, impossible to climb, and that is the very path this obstinate creature that I am will attempt. The ball, that enormous burden, is painfully hoisted step by step, with infinite precautions to a certain height, always backwards.

Sometimes I cannot hold it anymore and the ball will roll down. Again and again I will start afresh, till at last I am successful, or else understand the hopelessness of my efforts and perhaps I will take a smooth and easy road.

Or maybe someone will help me.

The one who will help me can be a partner but he can also be a robber.

To make one's own ball requires hard word and patience, to steal one ready-made is much easier. Some thieves go to work very craftily, other use violence.

I like these thieves.

If the thief has managed to get safely away with my ball – as I hope – then I can only resign myself to my loss, which I do with admirable fortitude.

I smile, I rub my cheeks, sniff the air, fly off and begin the job all over again. I admire and envy my character while I'm dreaming.

The sacred artist from Antwerp

Jan Fabre

Hans–Peter Feldmann

Subterranean Levitation

A series of adjoining, square, subterranean rooms: The walls and ceilings of the rooms are lined with polished blue marble. Each room measures 12'x12' with ceilings that are 15' high. Linked by doorway-sized openings, the rooms are flooded with water 3' deep. The smooth surface of the water, reflecting the blue of the marble, becomes the «floor» of a seamless 12' cube.
The only way to view these rooms is from above.
Hidden flush into each room's ceiling, a small hatch, which when opened, provides the sole source of light. The beholder looks down to see their own image, hovering in the colored surface of the water. From the floor where the viewer stands (the ceiling of the underground rooms), the hatch closes flush and disappears seamlessly. Each hatch represents the potential to peer into the subterranean spaces, regardless of whether the viewers are aware of the existence of the space below them, or simply walking mindlessly over them.

Teresita Fernández

A Dream, Perhaps

No dreams without sleep. Yet in contrast to dreams, sleep requires faith.

And the problem with faith is its lack of critical faculty. Do we not fall asleep every night with a reckless abandon that would be inexplicable, were it not that it rested on an ignorance of the dangers involved? Surely a consciousness that realizes its own ignorance has other things to think about than to sleep. Who can predict what will happen when the last gray bulb is extinguished at the blurry back of our heads?

«To enter sleep is to enter a slaughterhouse» (Cioran). Thus existence must seem to those deprived of faith in a well-intentioned Hypnos. Sleep is that space in which, for a handful of hours, man is reduced to a matter of flesh. All fret and reason, the insomniac never experiences such bodily disadvantage as clearly as when night descends. Again his brain is threatened by being washed of its perceptual plenitude, this residual hold on existence. Reluctant to being reprogrammed, he is thus kept awake by nocturnal unease – jolting, relentless, evermore numb.

While the rest of mankind snoozes with blissful wantonness, the sad few who remain sleepless must arrange themselves with the sorriest of companies: their own solitude. The vicious circle is complete when they cannot doze off, but at the same time have grown tired of the intercourse. Life emerges in all its feral continuity. To suppose that such experience furthers genius is a bohemian myth. Of course, sleeplessness only makes us encounter the wild, gray desolation at the heart of existence. But this may not be the worst of experiences. After all, an insomniac knows the score: as you make your bed, so you must lie on it.

Would it be a dream to imagine dreaming without the absurdity of sleep?

THE PRICE OF CIVILISATION OR ANIMALS DO NOT THINK OF MONEY

If I don't have any, I think about money. «I haven't got any now, and I need some. If only I had some I could do so many things. Make my dreams come true. At long last! After waiting for so long. Happiness itself. This is probably what happens to most people. Money is present at every table and in all dreams. Disguised to a greater or lesser extent. Without borders and without religion, quite simply better than any religion.

Only escape from the monetary system is an impoverishing prospect. Romantic, but not really dreamlike. This means that many should follow this approach. It should be difficult to discover it, because an exploit like this would lead you to the edges of society, like the poor. No, you should leave society. This immediately raises problems: where? Starting with the ground on which we stand, and what about our clothes? The sun does not shine for money. Even hunger would not be appeased by holy ideas. What about going into the forest? Living without a city? Making music on our own? Communes, Mormons, kibbutzim. The idea is not really attractive. And what if the children want money? Do we doubt the need for education? It's best to leave the practical question open.

If a free space exists inside us, money would fill it like water fills a bottle – recycled glass. The measurability of money is seductive: it allows us to distinguish ourselves from others, it promises to free us from our obligations, it makes us believe that, if we are on top, we will have space for our dreams. A real dream machine. A place where there is freedom for everyone, or at least for all who want it. We could save ourselves the trouble. Let us start immediately, or at least those who want to; let us get out of the monetary system and see what happens. As we set ourselves free, let us see what happens because of boredom in the absence of entertainment, how our problems take on a different look. It would be very interesting. I wonder what opportunities could be rediscovered by distinguishing ourselves again». This is my dream.

Urs Fischer

Surprise the World

I am getting dressed to go out. Someone phones and tells me the name, address and telephone number of the bar. I'll be there in 25 minutes.

I am sick of these preconceived urban forms based on the social structures of bygone days. I go out and start dreaming of another way of contacting people, a place, perhaps the only space in the town where, through art, we could still surprise each other.

Art needs freshness.

Imagine a meeting place where you don't know what you're going to do together. You would need to be flexible. You could no longer be a voyeur, a spectator: what is wanted is you, everything. You would never know what kind of things are going to happen, to connect you to others or even make you dependent on them.

You would never know if you are going out to a party or to discover a new way of dancing together, of swimming, of being silent together, or if touching will be important.

I will give you the illusion of a surprise.

We will arrange to meet there, like a secret society, without knowing what will be offered us, or even if we're wearing the right clothes.

A place where symbols are abolished, given over to the strangeness of *Atopia* (a place far away from your cognitive knowledge). The place where we will transform the social space by means of accidental sociability.

FROM TIME TO TIME I DREAM OF BEING MORE
INTELLIGENT

Giuseppe Gabellone

FACTORY CHIMNEY

The factory chimney was built as the centre of a traffic island.

It is twelve metres high and two metres in diameter at the bottom, tapering gradually as it gets higher; the diameter of the upper part is 1.2 metres. White smoke appears at established times. The external plastic surface of the factory chimney shows a clearly symmetrical masonry structure. It is red vermilion in colour. The ground of the traffic island is planted with short grass.

Technical data
The inner structure of the factory chimney consists of a steel frame anchored to the ground by a concrete plinth. A vermilion red plastic shell with a masonry structure is fixed onto this construction. This external shell is weather resistant. At the access of the factory chimney there is a sort of small tapestry coated door at the ground level. In the upper third of the factory chimney is a platform that can be reached using an inside ladder, and a mist machine will be installed on it.

Alberto Garutti

In this new house of yours: in the spacious entrance hall, I see the large, broad staircase; I follow the steps that rise to the first floor with my gaze until further above I see a wide, decorated ceiling.

At the centre of this ceiling, there is a rectangular cornice that once held a picture or fresco; above, beyond the ceiling, there is a small room.

I imagine the latter with a walled door, so that no one will be able to enter ever again and, in the middle of the floor, in the same position as the cornice in the ceiling beneath, a large hole. An empty rectangle.

I climb the stairs slowly and stop to gaze at the vertiginous opening that crosses the ceiling from wall to wall; I can just make out a portion of that small room that is inaccessible except through one's gaze. In the morning it is full of sunshine and the light slowly changes it during daylight; in the evening, it is dark and with the following dawn it reappears with a different meaning.

To be continued

Anna Gaskell

1. "CONTEXT"

Ten women are filmed in the following situations:
the women are nude, standing in a row, slightly bent down (leaning against a special stand) and pissing.

Monitors are put in a corridor placed above the heads of people, in a row, bent at 45 degrees, in a way that can be seen by visitors.
5-6 monitors at left side and 5-6 monitors at right side, making something like an arch.

Liquid is streaming down from the monitors and is collected by interconnected vessels at the bottom of the corridor and is streaming over a vane rotating a small generator. The generator supplies a small electric lamp.

2. "TRANSFERRING OF A SEARCH IN AN ENCLOSED SPACE"

I. On the territory of a military installation or unit (part of the system of the Ministry of the Defense of Bulgaria) in a region of the town of Botevgrad I direct the following action:
– a man, a specialist in finding water with a *baguetta* (a primitive wooden tool for discovering water) is searching for water on the territory of a military installation.
– a well is dug with a hand prospecting drill at a spot specified by the man.
II. Somewhere in the territory of Santa Fe, where a presentation (exhibition) is taking place, talks with the municipality are held asking for assistance to get permission (or to liaise in such a process) for negotiating with the owner of a territory of the Interior Ministry or a territory of another sort, but with an enclosed space, in order to gain normal access to it.

In close proximity of the fence from the inside portion of the "enclosed space" a search for water is undertaken and after the discovery of water the spot is drilled in depth with a prospecting geological drill. All actions in both places are filmed on S-VHS.

The above mentioned fence is pulled down and another fence is put up to sorround the drill (similar to a sleeve or an appendix) so it can be visited (accessed) by viewers. Inside this «sleeve» an alleyway of sentry-boxes will be built, in which both places will be displayed on monitors.

If you eat cheese, you dream
The harder the cheese, the better the dream

Gilbert & George

Having calculated the possibility that the theorem could not be performed in easy steps towards a clear resolution, I remembered that another group of people were working on a series of constructions that had caught my attention.

At that moment I realised that if I could prove their work to be correct then I too might be able to come to a solution. There was an intuitive logic at the heart of their incomplete work that felt close to the image I had at the end of my own calculations.

I set to work immediately and took five years proving that their work was correct. A mental side step could then be applied, moving across from their result to my guessed answer. Then, working backwards, I could prove the relation between my parallel solution and the initial theorem. A squared off O-shaped working technique.

Liam Gillick

A dinner maybe--a long and lingering dinner outside somewhere with fifteen or sixteen people from all over, people who like conversations, people who like telling stories, people who are simply fun to be with--people who I would like to have in one place for one day--

Jenny S., Detroit
Josephine P., London
Danny W., Atlanta
Alexandra T., Berlin
Anne W., Los Angeles
Willy C., Washington, D.C.
Jasmine A., Ann Arbor
Nicole M., Rotterdam
Sarah V. and Jon P., Charlottesville
Paul B., New York
Ellen C., wherever she is
Paul N., London
Frederico B., Sicily
Paula H., New York
Amy V., Jersey City

Like most dreams, something would be a little wrong with the picture--nobody would be able to hear--for a moment, for this one dinner, everyone would be deaf, everyone would have to write down everything they wanted to say, it would be a dinner where all the words would be on paper, and the paper would be everywhere--

Joseph Grigely

i was in another country, at another time, and i was in a museum. the only other person there was kasper, dressed in some of joseph beuys' old clothes. we embraced each other like long lost brothers and he told me that everything was fine. he disappeared and i walked around the wonderful museum.

the floors were not shiny.

they were old oak, found in another place, from another time, but looked happy in their new home. in another room, further away the floor was ash, in another room they were concrete, never shiny, but very happy.

the walls were white. they were straight walls that people could imagine were for pictures, or thoughts about pictures. they might be called working walls. these were different from the walking walls. walking walls were for people to walk along, or past, or both. they were the walls on the way from looking at pictures to thinking about pictures.

the walls were tall, so the rooms were tall.

the light in the rooms was beautiful and even. it all came from the top. there was no sense of where north and south light began and ended.

on the windows i could see that EVERY window had a mechanism to keep out the light if people wanted to be in the dark it was a beautiful, slow moving mechanism. it started to work. it looked like enormous venetian blinds turning slowly, but surely, from this way to that. i didn't know if i was watching or being watched. eventually the rooms darkened down. one by one.

and then i could smell the difference between the rooms more clearly as each floor had been polished with a different wax.

finally, i met another voice in the last room of the museum. the voice asked me what i was doing there. i told it that i was happy and the only thing that would make me happier would be to meet some other people with blue/green/brown eyes. the voice told me that if i tried hard enough then other people would come — whatever kind of people i liked. i told it that i thought museums were especially for children. of all ages. the voice asked me if children could understand art. i said it didn't matter, and that the best minds were in people of any age, who do feel affinity with 'understanding' anyway. children of any age do not need to understand everything, but they can always remember something.

that's why i like the museums in my dream. it was a space, and a place, that helped people to remember. and sometimes people would not remember anything for 5, 10 or 15 years. but that made it even better. like finding an old bottle of wine that someone had forgotten about, remembered and now it tasted better. oh, and i remember now. in one room in my dream, there was a real fire burning. it didn't matter that it was warm outside and inside.

and then i woke up.

1. Shooting a music video with Barry White in non-gravity space.

2. Floating upside down and «don't-change-the-colour-of-your-hair, love-you-the-way-you-are-kind-of-thing» in the background.

3. Perfect travellings of the camera, from point A to point B at a constant speed, without the need to hold your hands on the equipment, because of the zero gravity situation.

For Tatsumi and his Comrades - A Practical Dream

This proposal is for my technical assistant, Mr Tatsumi. He is a smoker. However, whenever he works with me, he is always inside a large museum which does not allow smoking. He must always go somewhere far off or just bear the uncomfortableness of not smoking for hours. Therefore I want to invent a smoke-filtration device, so people can freely relieve their addictions anywhere, even when people are in front of respected artwork. They can smoke nonchalantly while admiring the work. In addition, I want to create a Chinese herbal cigarette to completely solve this problem of smoking being bad for one's health, the environment, etc. So everything will be good.

The fact that the war in the Balkan area has boomed up again and that the misery of the rest of the world often blurs my rather positive vision of the future, I would've walked the path of Martin Luther King and others in dreaming of peace and harmony. But instead I will now note down a more personal and private dream. Perhaps this will contribute to a healthier and sounder place after all.

In 1982 I was sent to prison for refusing to do military service. I ended up at the psycho ward at Harlanda Prison in Gothenburg, together with a bunch of mentally disturbed wifekillers and bankrobbers, serving a one month sentence. Realizing that this would be a pretty dull and boring period I decided to declare this month a work of art. The piece would consist of two parts; a day project, contemplating the 5th Book of Moses from the Old Testament, and a night project, dealing with my heavily developed nightmares. My dream was thus to get rid of my horror dreams. As I had some time earlier stumbled upon a Malayan tribe technique of handling dreams, I decided to try it out: Always win when attacked. I feared my nightmares and I realized that they were in direct conjunction with my daily life and the fears that it brought along. Battling with my nightmares could be an autotherapeutic counselling.

The dreams that followed this decision were boring and I woke up several mornings in my cell feeling low, and a depression was slowly entering my mind. Then one night I had a classic nightmare. A certain dream that almost every human being has had:

«It is dark. A city a short time after some rain. Chilly. Not many street lights. A character appears in the distance coming towards me. A fearsome person. A huge man coming towards me. To crush me. To torture me and finally kill me. I turn around trying to outrun the threat. Legs moving slowly as if they gradually cease to function. The street turns to glue or melted asphalt. Feet get stuck. The horror is coming closer and closer. I'm losing speed. The pure fear sets in...»

Normally I would've woken up by now, sweating in terror. But:

«I realize the threat. I realize the dream I'm in and as I become aware of my goal to kill all enemies, I suddenly turn around. I face the horror. I walk towards this huge guy and I embrace him dearly».

I woke up in my cell with a smile on my face. I was happy. It was blissful.

Ever since that dream, I have never had another nightmare and this therapeutic function has altered my life. I'm not afraid of the dark anymore and I can and will confront anything that wants to be confronted. I live a good life.

There's only one small obstruction to this splendour. I have a new dream: I miss some of my dreams; some of my horror dreams and especially the hypnagogue condition where interaction by will is possible. I want some of it back.

Thomas Hirschhorn

I don't wonder about the function of contemporary art. I don't even wonder about the function of my work. But I do firmly believe that it is absolutely necessary that my work does not function. And of course I also think the same in relation to contemporary art, and art in general. What irritates me about the idea of «functions» is the academic hope for new criteria. But it is precisely this that has not existed now for quite a while. I don't believe that the «art of providing service», «informative art», «documentary art» will make a decisive contribution that can help us to escape from the hurly-burly of consumption. As far as I am concerned, this is only possible «for oneself».

I must focus everything on being free with «myself». Of course, this won't work because I am a paradox. However, I don't want to force this paradox. I want to try much more to compare myself freely with it, try to understand it as resistance, use it as something whole, clean, something belonging to myself. This is my mission as an artist. I know that the word «mission» is not well thought of. In spite of this it continues to be used in the field of art because there are «impossible missions», to counter the functions that must rule out the impossible. I am not a theoretician or a philosopher, I am a worker, an artist, a soldier.

I do not fight for myself, I owe my victory to others. I believe in energy, not in quality. I lower the thoughts of quality; only energy counts! I always bear in mind the wonderful philosophical affirmation made *à propos* the question about the meaning of philosophy - «Philosophy may bring sorrow». I love Robert Wasser, Thomas Bernhard and Ingeborg Bachmann.

you
know
that
awful
feeling,
where
you
wake
up
in
the
morning
and
you
just
know
you've
murdered
someone

Damien Hirst

A Dream...
Which repeats through centuries already ...
a dream of peace, everywhere...
just peace and quietness, sheltered, social justice,
equal rights for everyone, between man and woman,
between different ethnical and political groups
we know it is just a dream —
Is dreaming strongly connected to a wish?
Is this utopian condition just by dreaming possible?
It will never happen, there is too much egoism, too much
presumption...
How to reach this fata morganic state, with all this history of the 20th century behind and the actual happening
beside — in front —
...having lost the link to political ideologies...
...a dream of a «social paradise» on earth, not in heaven,
...without existential suffering...
in a protected nature, with a possibility for animals to live
in their needed environment,
for plants to grow...
But will it make happiness? (This is another question,
because it never existed...)
an old, old dream, never realised......
when do we start to share work, to approximate payment
in order to reduce the gap between the ones who have nearly nothing and the ones who are able to live in plentiful
surplus...

Christine und Irene Hohenbüchler

...when does this responsibility for each other replace the status of an expensive car, materialistic goods...

...is it easy to demand these changes in the global order from the position of a «protected artist» in Austria?...

a dream between a nap and this writing...

The camouflage dream

...sitting in my small woodhouse,

dominant colouring brown spruce-wood

I dreamed, sitting on the brownish sofa, to adapt suddenly its colour

...with an additional cap on my head which I can pull over my face ...prevalent feeling of a big relief. To have the possibility to disappear, just to be not on the surface anymore...

...when I have got my kids, I lost my dreams...

strangely, but since then I hardly dreamed anymore (maybe because I always get waked up and do not wake up on my own?)

The real kidnapped the fantastic? ...Surely I have become much more realistic since the births of the two children. Which has its good sides in order to get a parent but sometimes in sentimental moments I miss the grotesque moments of the dreams...

Carsten Höller

I have no more dreams,
Because dreams are all I have

«A palace. There is some ironware on the roof. The eighth piece has been struck by lightning. Its colour has turned deeply golden from silver. God says, it's a re-incarnation».

Is this a dream?

From the sea the land is frieze and scroll. The rock island whose surface is obscured occasionally by greenery is chalky and light in color. Round and well and generously spaced bushes grow ideal from its earth; they are a dense green, almost too dense for the green to be perceptible. Each bush is filled out by its black shadow to a perfect circular symmetry. These bushes and bush-shadows guide my gaze as I stare continuously at the changing view.

The island landscape is composed of washed-out ochre rubble broken up intermittently by large and weathered rock outcroppings, —and the sense of dust compressed into mass, —and the sense of a thing that has once been another thing, —and the sense of a hardness impermeable and ungiving and cooked up a long time ago. The mostly cloudless blue sky assures a sunlight of relentless and unchanging intensity. No shadow except the small shade of each bush perforates the dense light. As I squint my eyes from the water, I imagine the reality of this island baking without end in the bright heat.

The island is still. This simple fact is the dominant presence and counterpoint to the turbulence of surrounding ocean and sky. The land mass appears to end or begin at the water. It is an ending or a beginning in the form of a line. On one side of it crowds a static mass and on the other the sea laps and merges.

In the foreground of my view the tumultuous manner of the ocean plays out. The surface heaves chaotically, undulating without repetition everywhere. White caps lick at its very-blue self. Troughs of rolling space submerge and mingle with crests. In the mid-ground of the view the water flattens improbably into a plane and line and an idea of the bottom of the island.

The line is level and flat and straight and perfect in the manner these adjectives suggest—perfect also in the way that perfect things can be.

As the taxi moves along in the water the island conveys its linear changing and repeating and constant form to me. As I watch the island slowly unfurl it is continuously changing in a radical and complete manner though the changes *as they occur* are imperceptible. I feel my anxiety at not being able to see them. It is the experience of losing control—of a sudden closing in. It is the experience of something escaping just as I am about to recognize it. I feel the anxiety of a thing disappearing slowly; of its change attenuating to a visibility one increment beyond my ability to see it.

As the taxi moves along in the water the island conveys its linear changing and repeating and constant form to me. The frieze of it is constant—an elongated shape further extended by these long afternoon hours taxiing beside the island elevation. The frieze of it is marked by a leit motif of ochre outcroppings. The scroll of it is the island unfurling as I cruise along; the scroll of it is the repetition happening in different places, making each repetition different. The island unscrolling becomes a short narrative with various and unique incidents interrupted by unchanging recurrence. Each recurrence adds to the mass, making an island circumnavigable in one hour when taken at a reasonable, not swift, and not dawdling pace.

Returning to the beginning, the island-frieze ends, forming a repetition that is the final difference–a relapse in view from a different point of view, totaling the island into interval.

Island Frieze
April 8, 1994/99
Hydra, Greece

Fabrice Hybert

I dreamt that the whole world refused to make peace. People preferred looking after their bonsais or gardens and I desperately tried to free the bonsais by planting them in the ground. In order to make it easier to free them, I suggested planting the bonsai in La Serrie: the valley of bonsais.

I also dreamt that Céline Dion was having talks with Milosevic.

Chuangtse once dreamed that he became a butterfly. He was so happy to fly around and thus he wasn't aware that he was Chuangtse. However when he woke up, he was Chuangtse himself. Who dreamed of who? Was this a dream of a butterfly in which she transmuted to Chuangtse?
Or did Chuangtse dream that he transmuted to a butterfly? He was completely lost.

This is a famous story by Chuangtse known as «A dream of a butterfly».
Any causality relationship is just an illusion.
No distinction exists between I and you.
Every distinction changes from time to time.
This is the world view underlying the story.

One day, a computer (may not be a von Neumann type) will dream that he becomes me.
Or I will dream that I become a computer (process).
I will be happy to fly around all over the world through networks and won't be aware that I am surely myself.
And may I not come to recognize who simulates who, I or a computer?
May be both.

This is I or artificial life may dream of.

Takashi Ikegami

Ann Veronica Janssens

PILOT STUDY FOR «FOUNTAIN» IN MIDDELBURG

«A drop of water that might fall after an hour or evap-
orate or leave a minuscule quantity of material, mostly
lime, which would lead to the formation of a stalactite.
By landing on a surface, the drops could also form a
stalagmite in the same way».
(This process would be very long term, lasting centuries).

I am not yet sure how to accomplish this project. I
should return to Middelburg, visit the square, invent a
technique for channelling the water, and choose a site...
The whole thing still needs to be thought through!

Daydreams... Like nightdreams are narratives which lead to satisfaction by representing the fulfilment of wishes. I'm lonely and I need to be with someone tonight. The car drives up to the curb, we stop in the night of black and white, he peers into the window. I wind the window only a quarter of the way down. A gun is being hoisted down his throat, he turns to me making his hands restrain the other hand.

CUT TO his face in sharp close-up pressed against the glass. his light brown skin is reddened against the smooth glass.
«Desire was like a double death of our mingled breath, unknown strange perfume in a naked room».

Running now with him behind he drives the light shine blinded me to his direction I ran into the direction of a horse head in the street with a carriage behind its door open I step into a house where from the entrance I see a letter yet to be finished written at the desk my hand stretches out over exaggerated distanced to pick up the fountain pen. It reads – their swinging bodies, that camouflages of skin needs to be seen – I finish the letter only you can tell what I want the ink which flows turns from blue to red filling half the room I open the door the garden is beautiful I can see the black servants tending its lawn. We make polite conversation ignoring both our nakedness.

Isaac Julien

MEMORIAL TO A LOST CIVILIZATION

The Russian Revolution, ushering in the «era of Socialism», is considered to be an extremely important event of the 20th century. The end of this «era of Socialism» during the end of the 1980's could be considered a no less important event of our century. But totalitarianism exciting the political arena in Eastern Europe and the territory of the former Soviet Union does not signify merely that a viscous and heavy fog has suddenly dissipated into thin air and underneath the shining cloudless ground of democracy has been revealed once again. It is still preserved in the consciousness and subconscious of people who survived totalitarianism and experienced its influence personally. However, it is equally clear that totalitarianism did not simply fall upon humanity as a political system from nowhere, but rather its «seeds» live and exist in each of us, and for the sake of the future, this cannot be forgotten or ignored.

This is why the creation of a unique memorial to Soviet totalitarianism is so important. However, this will be a memorial not to its victims who perished in the camps – that memorial has yet to be created and erected on the very territory where all of this occurred. This will be a memorial to those who survived in that world, but with a consciousness deformed under the influence of propaganda and the incessant mental repression, which in extreme forms lead to the emergence of the consciousness of the «Soviet person» with his false enthusiasm and doublethink. This is a memorial to Soviet life in its everydayness, in its ordinary «daily existence», where in particular, the natural connections of a person with the world, with others, with his own soul were violated in every trifle, influenced by all-pervasive fear. This is a memorial to the various forms of survival of «the humane in an individual» – this survival at times took the form of strange, hideous, fantastic, and at other times funny and endearing projects that a person juxtaposed to the most «beautiful» and bloodiest project in the history of humanity, i.e. the creation of Communist Paradise on this Earth. But after all, this relates to any person in any society, not only in a totalitarian one, where society in any form deforms the human personality, forcing him to subordinate and change his own human nature.

The dreams I have are usually ones of anxiety, fear, or seeking for comfort – looking for a lap in which to lie. They do not directly suggest themselves as large-scale projects. These dreams find their way into the work, but generally on a small and manageable scale – some charcoal and paper, a video projector.

In terms of ideal projects, there are larger pieces – which have to do with open air projection, a combination of singing and projected image, and projections in other unexpected found spaces. But these always start off amorphously and in the making both consolidate their form and find their subject matter and meaning. To describe a coherent project is like writing a proposal – even though it may be the truth, it always sounds false. To try to enumerate them in advance is as hopeless as saying «describe the dream you are going to have tonight». The most I can do is describe some of the elements I would like around the bed, waiting to hold onto extrusions and remnants of the dream. Film, camera, 3 projectors, some old motor cars (to use their windscreens as projection screens), a composer and his piano, and the singer patiently next to him on the piano stool – waiting.

William Kentridge

Koo Jeong-a

I would like to see someone
who has a piece of moving cloud
around Torino.

and make sense of

ousss
ousss ousss ousss

ousss

inside.

A HOUSE FOR THE FUTURE

In the last two years, I have had the opportunity to travel and spend some time abroad thanks to scholarships or programmes for artists in residence. Through architecture, I have tried to relate to what was around me, and to orientate myself, concentrating upon the representation of the architecture, and registering sensations that anonymous spaces or those built by famous architects suggested to me.

I would like to follow this avenue further, and in «Dreams» I aim to go even further. I would like to produce a work – if possible, a «documentary» – in Brasilia, the «city of the future» designed by Lucio Costa and Oscar Niemeyer in the fifties and inaugurated in 1960.
Like Chandigarh which I have visited and was built in India almost at the same time by Le Corbusier, with whom Niemeyer worked, Brasilia is the expression of a utopia.

It is said that Brasilia springs from a dream by Don Bosco, the Italian saint born in 1815 and the founder of the Order of Salesians: «...between parallels 15 and 20 there was a long and wide depression in the vicinity of a lake. Thus spoke a voice, over and over again; ″...when they come to explore the riches buried in these mountains, here will rise the promised land of milk and honey, of inconceivable wealth...″».

It seems that the city, as a result of the way it was born and has developed, lives and is protected more in its fantastic dimension than in the real one.
It is just because the initial project proved unsuitable and the dream has not yet come true that it is all the more precious and in some way still possible.
The city corresponds to an imaginary, abstract architecture, to a possibility rather than its real image, and it is precisely its least visible character that I would like to record.

Luisa Lambri

John Latham

«On band Q we are a plague organism
But on band S we show up as seed germ of the Sun».

John Latham from Flat Time

THE TRANSVERBERATION OF TEODOLINDA:

Plötzlich O sah ich
Karl Marx leibhaftig vor mir stehn.

His burning face, enflamed,
burned with passion.
He grasped
a sickle & a golden hammer

whose tip
shone with sparks of fire.

It seemed to me
that Karl was plunging
the tip of the sickle
repeatedly
into my heart
and thrusting it into the depths
of my bowels.

And the blade
sliding out of my body, seemed
to drag me with it.

Und da überkam Teodolinda
grenzenlose Begeisterung
für den Klassenkampf!

And the pain was so great
that I moaned,
and so excessive was the sweetness
of this pain
that... one cannot want it to end.

i've always had the same wish whenever i visit venice. i would like to experience it the way dirk bogarde did at the opening of visconti's «Death in Venice», the film based on mann's great novel. bogarde is on a boat and entering venice from seaside. the atmosphere is grey and sanguine. the voyage is languorous but then venice opens up and its beauty and fragility only makes the heaviness of the mood all that more saturating. like all dreams, the end is an idea; it is the passage that is real. also like all dreams, nightmares and regrets lurk behind every turn. as we all know dreams can collapse into nightmares very readily. in fact, they are interlinked.

in my dream of venice, i arrive from the sea and the day is cold and layered in fog. i cannot see venice but i know it is impending. i can sense it in my bones. it is very easy to slip into a kind of aphasia, a kind of deep trance. the noise of the small motor, the splash of the sea would lull me very easily. during these moments, i see people running and screaming in fear. i also see slaves tucked into cramped quarters on their way to the americas. i see old and young struggling to escape to a less violent place; many of them do not make it. i see the horror of conrad's «Heart of Darkness», another story of a boat trip. i think that «Death in Venice» is not so separable from conrad's heart of darkness in many ways.

every so often, the sound of seagulls and the smell of the sea's brine would realert me to venice. and i would be lulled again only this time by thoughts of its impossible beauty and perfection. it is what gives the world hope, and as in henry james' «the Wings of the Dove», it would be a splendid place to die.

Ken Lum

White wine

a small black and white image of his face could be made into a dot-to-dot sequence of xy axis points, then converted into 4 bit code, then translated into the 4 proteins of DNA, constructed, and inserted into the junk DNA of some grape plants. On a hot hillside grow the vines for a few years, look after them, then after 3 years at the least you can start to harvest this fruit which might contain the image hidden in its structure so you can make some wine containing the drawing. Where would her face go to when you got drunk?

Christina Mackie

Masami Akita

As far back as the Edo era, the artificial Fuji (FUJIZU-KA) was a heavenly gift that saw the light from faith in Mt. Fuji. Small mountains as miniatures of the original Mt. Fuji were built during a flourishing cultural period in 55 places in Edo city. Their shapes are not too similar to the original Mt. Fuji. If you are close to one of them, it looks just like a rugged mountain, but the fact that it is made in part of melted rocks brought from Mt. Fuji barely illustrates the reason for its name.

There are two Fujizuka near my house. One is called Komagome-Fuji, the other Jujoh-Fuji. Both are famous, but specially Jujoh-Fuji gives a strange sensation due to its location in the middle of a residential area.

I wish I could have one in my garden as well.

I was asleep lying on my right side on a small couch, legs bent. I opened my right eye. The horizontal line of the floor of the room ran parallel to my body – a correct perception. I then sat up. As I sat up, the line of the floor, the entire room, remained parallel to my body. The floor line of the room was now vertical. I understood this as a split in my visual perception and my physical sensations. My left eye would not open. I laid back down and closed my right eye. I seemed to drift into a dream in which I was in a village in Africa. The men and women of the village were dancing. They danced by jumping up and down. A man danced in front of me. At one point during the dream I opened my right eye. The floor of the room ran parallel to my body as it should if I was lying down. But in my left eye or on my left side, I continued to view the dancers. I was perceiving two separate events both with different axis. On the right side – the room – the floor was horizontal. On the left side the village was vertical. Both seemed correct in that I was lying down in one and standing in the other.

I suddenly shifted to being awake sitting on the couch, both eyes perceived the room correctly. I went to the front door and deliberately felt the door handle thinking this was a good way of testing whether I was awake or dreaming. I clearly remember feeling the door handle. I was satisfied that this was proof that I was awake. I opened the door to look outside. I then woke up on the couch lying on my right side.

Paul McCarthy

In my dreams; I dream that my memory is erased, every time I see, smell, hear and taste beauty.
Joy is repetition

MY DREAM IS... To tell you the truth, I do not have any future dreams. All I want is what I always wanted: to be here and now and do, and help and protect what the present time is bringing out very naturally. But this, of course, gets me so involved in so many things, that I find very little time left for myself. Thus, of course, I wish, – but this is not a dream, – that I could find time to complete all my unfinished films; find time to edit all my written diaries from 1950-1999; and find time to visit all my good friends in France, Japan, Italy, Austria, Germany and everywhere, and have wine and sake with them. Thus, I wish, – this is not a dream, only a wish, – that somebody who loves cinema and finds as much ecstasy in it as I do, gives Anthology Film Archives enough money to establish an Endowment for it so I could free myself from all the money raising work and do my own work. But I think I have one big problem: my dreams and wishes of what I have to do for the others and my dreams and wishes of what I want to do for myself are totally and inseparably woven together... Ah, I almost forgot my biggest dream: I dream that someday I could afford to eat and drink as much as I want, like normal people do. This has been my dream from childhood, and I am still dreaming it.

Jonas Mekas

If you write the word REVER (DREAM) in French backwards

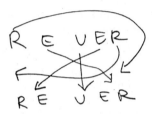

...you get "REVER"...There's a lot to dream about...
A word that means the same whether it is written backwards or forwards!
You only know the night's dreams when you awake, afterwards, when you have pieced them together, you distorted them...
Whilst it is important for me to daydream, in fact I can dream that I am an animal, woman, doctor, child, artist... Waking dreams are active, full of life and they keep me in training.

Annette Messager

I CAN'T BREATHE ANYMORE (4:550)

OUR POOR ROOMZ R2 BIG / 2 SM:ALL SO, I CAN'T HIDE MYSELF ~ I CAN'T FIND MYSELF HERE. LISTEN 2 ME=LISTEN ME: ME – DON'T SPEAK 2 ME = DON'T SPEAK ME: ME. U SUX MY WORLD BY THE LIPS OF "2 WANT" – THE PUMP OF THE WILL AND MAY-B IT WILL B. CLEANED SPAZE WITHOUT REST. HYGIENIC SOLIDARITY. U GOES. HERE IS NOT PLACE 4 ME – SO, THERE IS NO PLACE IN ME 4 UNDERSTANDING U. I AM LOOZING MY SELF HERE = THE ROOMZ 4:2 WHERE XTCZ LAX NRG – NEVROTIK WALLZ SKREEMIN' 4 DESTRUKTION. SEMI-SPHERIK FREEDOOM. METAPHYSIQUE REALIZM WITHOUT MEDITATION. LOVE AFTER LOVE. STILL LOVE / STILL LIFE. WEEPING NIPPLEZ, XHOSTED BREASTS = THIS IS THE TYRANNY OF RELATION. YOUR EGOIZM IS PUZZLED IN BRUTAL SILENCE LEAVING THE GUILT 2 B SHEARED. I HATE THIS CITY.
I REALLY CAN'T STAND THIS VILLAGE ANYMORE. TENTACLES COVERED BY POWDER OF SUNDAY GARDENZ. TOXIK MINDZ OF RUNNING NEIGHBOROUGHS. WHO AM I FINALLY? MESS IS BUILDING MY IDENTIFICTION. I DON'T WANT WATT I WOULD LIKE 2 MEANZ THAT I WANT WATT I WANT BUT DON'T WANT 2 LOOZE THE THINX WHICH I WILL LOOZE IF I WILL GET IT. U JUMPED IN MY SPEECH 4 THE 3RD TIME. THIS IS 2 MUCH AND I HAVE 0 REEZON 2 FOLLOW THIS VACUUMED STEREOLOGUE. EVERYTHINK NOTHINK. (U R LIKE BROTHER 2 ME) VACUUM OF KAOZ. ABTRAKT AIMZ – FUCK THEM ALL OFF. BORING KILLING IN NOWAYOUT SHACKLEZ. INNOCENT CHAIN OF COHERENCEZ. FENZE OF CIRCUMSTANCEZ. DYING DOMINO FX. R:H 4 HELP. LIVE 4 ME OR ERAZE ME 4 GOOD. IS THIS THE INDIKATION OF OUR DECAYDE? DEEP DARK PRO:CESS.P(00)L 99. ONLY SLEEP WITH ME BUT DON'T FALL ASLEEP. I FEEL DANGER OF THIS COLD SECURITY. THE PRESENT DANGER OF FOG AND DIZZY SULTER OF FINGERZ – RUSTY FROM SUGAR OF COUNTING. I NEED THE SUPPORT WHEN YOU PLAY THE HEADLINER. U ACTZ AS THE SEA SON OF THE BEACH. BLEACH YOUR SANDZ DOWN 2 THE GROUND. BURNDIE. DON'T LEAVE ME ALONE. B HERE BUT LEAVE ME 2 B ON MY OWN. PRAKTIKAL REZULTZ – I DO NOT FOKKKA CARE'BOUT THEM. KRUEL. I NEED YOUR SIMPLE FRANK ASSISTANCE. HEAVY PRESSURE WITHOUT PLEASURE. ALL OF ALL ROOMZ OF ALL 4 ALL.1. 4 ALL AND NOBODY 4. 1. I DIDN'T EAT BUT I DON'T FEEL LIKE 2. TAKE A STROOONG PILL 2 HARD SLEEP CAUSE I WANNA B ALONE TONIT – IN THIS BAD DESIGNED – HEAVY FUTURE.
IN BETWEEN ASTRIDEAD ROOMZ U SOX MY WORLD 4:2 WITHOUT FLOOR.

Boris Ondreička

Gabriel Orozco

I would like to live long enough to see Mexico win the
World Cup.

Dream N. 9

never a practical man-powered means of flying was
made.
The only things that flew, with man-power, where
giant monsters, standing in a Langas waiting for special weather and a crew to coax them on their way.
Institution things, made by rule and academism, to
prove some theoretical fact, to win some cheap prizes
and with no original idea what-so-ever in them.
Imagine a big propeller on your back and a hand pow-
ered mechanism, light weight about 3 kg and leaving
your feet all free to run around. That and a bag with a
kitewing.

There would be no wheels, chariot, tail or rudder the
total weight of it with wing could be 20 kg.
The pilot will look like a hunter skier with a big gun on
his back.

Panamarenko

Jennifer Pastor and I have lived together for several years. She often helps me with my sculpture projects. I've come to depend on her eye as well as her hand. She often tells me her dreams. Here's one about me and her.

It is a sunny day on the edge of town. She is sitting outside on a hill on the spacious grounds of an old convent, preparing to eat an elaborately laid out lunch. I am briskly walking toward her on a long road, the old red brick convent just behind her. Walking alongside me is a three legged dog.

She is upset that I mistake her for a nun. I shout «Hey sister work a miracle on my dog!» She is disgusted I don't see the miracle has already occurred, in that my three legged dog is walking beside me.

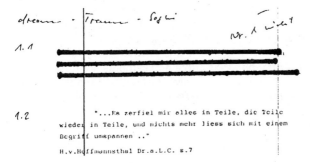

«I fell into pieces, the pieces fell into other pieces, and nothing could be embraced any longer in a concept ...»

H.v. Hoffmannsthal Dr. A.L.C. p. 7

I need air, I grab my board (more a bodyboard or swimmer's kickboard than surfboard) and head for the surface through the oily, alcoholic wet ether. Fortunately, it's a long, slow trip: by the time I surface I'm clear-headed.

There's a wrestling ring atop, bobbing and floating on the water. The scene seems set more for a cock-fight than a staged WWF-type phony «exhibition». Real wrestling, real fans, real blood: betting and brawling-an entertainment, not a sport. Dick Lane, Jeff Walton, Judo Gene, they're all there–this is where they hang on the days off when the scripts and cameras are no-shows.

The fight managers are introduced–Freddie Blassie and John Tolos, followed into the ring by their own. One is a blond, affectionate All-American boy (I do not remember his name), who gets a scattering of applause and wolf whistles–he's the crowd favorite. Goliath (pronounced Go-lee-ought in Spanish)–the one-time tag-team partner of Black Gordman – is intro'd next. When Jimmie Lennon announces him as «...and claiming to be from New Mexico!» the peanut gallery rains down bottles and cups of beer and piss on the ring and ring-side.

As the bell sounds the grapplers come out kicking and swinging and both are soon covered in blood, sweat, and piss. Referee Red Shoes Dugan goes to a two-count a number of times on both fighters. At one point he is on the verge of deducting a full point from the pretty boy for taking a foreign object from out of his trunks, when Goliath, out on nowhere! digs deep and goes to his own bag of tricks, and in a move that leaves even the hardened veteran commentator Dick Lane at a loss for words ("Whoaaaah Nellie!" indeed), bites his foe's balls clean off!

I awake from my dream with tubes down my nose and throat, and up my urethra, begging for morphine and TV.

I dreamt that whilst walking I came across a large black dog lying by the edge of the road; seeing me approach, it raised its head and looking at me, said: «Hello, Michelangelo», to which I replied, «How did you know my name was Michelangelo?» Its reply came back: «My name is Michelangelo».

Michelangelo Pistoletto

Paola Pivi

TRAVEL THROUGH SPACE WITH MY DAUGHTER

The Dream of Syntopy

Look at a globe – the globe we live on. You turn it around and you see the different countries marked with different colours. Some are small, some are very big-but they are clearly separated indicating the isolation of the people living within its borders. Look at another globe – no countries are indicated, just mountains, deserts, rivers, and above all the ocean!
There are no people. We look at this globe as being not inhabitated, it is an object looked at from outside. But obviously it is a globe we are living on. It is our place, our Ba (as the Japanese say) or our Ort (as the German say).
Well, I do not want to speak for somebody else – it is certainly my place (UNDERLINE MY PLACE PLEASE) although I obviously don't own it.
How is it my place? Because of the nework of friends I have all over the place. The togetherness of places «the syn-topy» makes it my place.
Independent of living in a jungle – in mountains or at a river – in cities – in countries of different political systems, different race, different religion, different history, different gender, different age, different wealth – we together, my friends an myself, are one – of many – (potential & real) networks that actually hold this globe together. People sitting only at one (PLEASE UNDERLINE ONE) place, with one prejudice, one historical knowledge, one form of art, one language, one tunnel vision, they might be causal to ruin this place. But the dream of syntopy is to havethese networks – every one of us - which in an overlapping manner put net over net - which iteself are internetted- to make this my place, our place.
Thus, look at my globe with the pictures of friend coming from different continents, different professions, different pastimes, different you name it.....

Ernst Pöppel

Emilio Prini

CARI OBRIST E BONAMI VI VOGLIO TANTO BENE E
MI DICO VOSTRO FIGLIO AFFEZIONATISSIMO
EMILIO

(a little telegram by Emilio Prini)

dreams?

these dream things seem to be the emotional scan
disk of the mind.

Jason Rhoades

I dreamt that I was the editor of a pornographic booklet publishing house. The office is as large as a football stadium. It is like being in Tokyo, although none of my female colleagues smoke. The largest rooms are the toilets, which are twice the size of the office itself and fully decorated. Every day we publish a booklet describing a new sexual practice. Today's protagonists wear two clitorises on each thumb, and they poke them into their ears. When they are overcome by tiredness, they prepare the bed; the buttercup seed that pops out of the thumb germinates in the earwax and the man's head explodes. The booklet explodes as well. I escape disguised as a bee. The morning sun shines on the wet and juicy green field. I buzz from one yellow flower to another in the middle of this brutal green and extreme blue. The newly milked milk smokes because it is so hot; a sort of hurricane is blowing in the bucket, shaped like a Louis XV curl, 50 cm high. In the wood behind, a young girl is hurtling on a truck along the bumpy riverbed. The heavy vehicle swerves away from the gravel, and the girl just manages the window slit.

I pull her away from the riverbed and hold her on my breast. Her mud-matted hair dirties my stiff white shirt. The girl disappears under my armpit until just her hands can be seen. The sun shines through her thin fingers, making them look orange.

Crying like a chained dog, I am dancing in a disco; it looks like our house. My tears shine in the coloured light. I am not ashamed or even frightened and I jump around like a monkey. The soles of my feet slip on the floor wet with tears. This makes the dance even quicker.

My body hovers horizontally to rest. From every direction, the persons who were dancing with me fly upwards and caress me with their small cold hands to console me, all over my body which burns because of the salty water. The intimacy of the places does not indicate any special relationship with those who are consoling. After having cried enough, I am free to choose my new identity. I think that I will become like you.

Ugo Rondinone

I'm standing under water in a corner of my room and wearing diving goggles without a snorkel.

The water is murky and my mask fogged up so that I can only see the blurred contours of the fish swimming apathetically back and forth between bed and chair and window. I sit down on the floor and wait for something to happen, and just as I am about to drop off, a skate comes gliding my way, a huge flat thing the size of a garbage–can lid. I see that its tiny eyes are staring at me and I raise my arms, whether to catch it like that or ward it off, I don't remember now, but for a moment, before it turns away, I touch it and then the skate almost seems to be lying in my arms; I can feel its muscles tensing and than relaxing, and under the skin, the beat of something against my arms.

I don't want to let it go anymore.

For a long time I've wondered if public transport couldn't be overhauled by creating on all the major (and even not so major) thoroughfares of a city a kind of continuous flow of small, bubble-like electric tramways that one could get on and off at will. There would be no waiting, no limit of hours, and there would be no need to worry about the destination of a particular tram line, since one could simply hop off whenever one needed to. Of course, the design of the individual bubble-like trams would be very important for the aesthetics of the city and the trams should be able to stop for brief moments without interfering with the general flow of all trams, so that those who have difficulty getting on and off can take their time. Also, I think it would be important that each «bubble» seat from four to eight people (if this is not enough there's always another bubble just behind!) and have space for packages, and perhaps little tables for reading and writing as well, for those who are travelling longer distances. Finally, there should be a system for changing from the slow continuous line of bubble-like trams, to a more rapidly moving set of continuous trams.

Israel Rosenfield

Bojan Sarcevic

Dreaming that one refuses bread in order to give it to his own children and that this would be a joy.

Thomas Schütte

I was walking to M.O.C.A., which looked more like L.A.C.M.A. from the outside, surprised to find out they were opening my survey show. The park-like grounds had rolling yellow tiled walkways with little skid resistant bumps and some employees were grumbling about the difficulty of setting up the modernist steel sculpture they had been assigned to on such an uneven surface. Off the path in a tar-pit-like pond, a woman performed, jogging in a costume that was like a cement version of the Venus of Willendorf from the hips down. Further, a group of costumed hippies collapsed in a pile. One was like a rastafarian elephant with inflated black Nikes, another like god on stilts, another in a playboy's outfit (white shut, black bow tie). It was hilarious and I recommended it to other passers-by. I showed Cameron a dummy version of the catalogue. Rosamund had an apartment/gallery in the museum, most of which was a low ceilinged wide rectangle like some 60's movie set. She didn't have my work up like she was supposed to, but instead big glossy blowups of details from Marnie's hamster collages! Made my way to the show, but it turned out to be simply displays of 50's and 60's pop ephemera, like screens devoted to old cheap sci-fi kids shows working as space dividers. Reading tables and wall displays featured a cutesy cartoon alien sort of as a guide or symbol of my work and sound track music blared out. Different sized felt squares lined the floor of the halls made out of room dividers. It scared me to think this was all my work had amounted to. My aunt and uncle were in line and I couldn't remember if I'd invited my parents. I climbed up a ramp made of cushions, that my sister was at the top of.

Jim Shaw

Boundless; genetic hedonists and aesthetes

As a genetic aesthete and hedonist my dream is for a boundless space in which genetic aesthetes will be full members of society. Genetic hedonists do not have to be born with the hedonist gene, the gene can be injected as long as the recipient declares him/herself to be a genetic hedonist. Governments will allocate funds specially for card carrying aesthetes and hedonists. All aesthetes who have declared their lack of inclination for work will be registered for special treatment immediately as long as they are willing to abide by strict rules:

1. A genetic hedonist never gets out of bed before 11am in the morning.
2. A genetic hedonist must always make love on impulse.
3. A genetic hedonist has no hate gene and therefore lacks the ability to be disrespectful towards people.
4. A genetic hedonist has no need for self defence since they are highly valued by society.
5. A genetic hedonist is above the law.
6. A genetic hedonist must dress outrageously well at all times.
7. A genetic hedonist will transform the fortune of designers of their choice simply by wearing their clothes.
8. A genetic hedonist must never work except in circumstances where a thing of beauty has to be created; this must never be described as work.
9. A genetic hedonist in the same room with you will make you fall in love with all your neighbours immediately regardless of their cultural background.
10. A genetic hedonist owns a share in every corporate organisation.
11. A genetic hedonist is never moral.
12. A genetic hedonist must seek pleasure relentlessly.

Yinka Shonibare

Andreas Slominski

Do not let your left hand know what your right hand is doing. Walking next to the pony is different from riding it.

«I was walking across a parking lot.
On a small lawn behind the parked cars I saw some-
thing moving.
When I stopped to get a better look I realized that there
were two wolves mating.
The one on top was eating the other.
He continued to do so until the female wolf was cleaned
to the bone when he picked her up and I saw that she
had the skeleton of a fish with the head of a wolf.
Then I continued to look for my car and drove off».

Rudolf Stingel

Dream of being a snake

When I looked, I was a snake. Gazing around from a quite lower point of the bush, there was my friend, another snake (I am not sure about its sex), and the sun was shining around us. Anyway, I was sleepy.
At this time, I found out for the first time how snakes could be so sleepy during the daytime.
While dozing, someone was rustling along the bush on the other side.
My snake friend cried to me. «Watch out, and run away!»
I thought that my friend must be a female, then.
At that moment, an animal like weasel or fox was staring at me. I got a little panicky, thinking I might be eaten, for the first time. And from the other side, my friend was crying out «Run away!»
I hurriedly tried to escape but I could hardly move forward.
It was utterly peculiar.
I had not walked yet since I became a snake.
And I don't know how to go forward.
That big animal had munched me while I was trying to move...
It was the first time I was eaten. Surprisingly, it wasn't painful at all and even bracing.

Next year, I realized this dream as a beautiful folly with nineteen connected bicycle-like tools which can hardly be ridden. However it is supposed to be as if it can not be ridden alone but can be ridden when it is connected.

After that I had dreamed dreams so far.
Some dreams were realized on earth by my art work.
The rest are lost in the jungle.
In the jungle where I lost days and nights, out of civilization, I'm just dreaming.
Dreaming is folly but dreaming is my business.

I had a dream.
I was dancing with my friends on the square when the sun was setting. Our shadow was long on the ground. It was an ordinary, everyday scene inside the colours of the arena. But something unusual happened to me. The speed of my dancing feet accelerated and enabled me to dance as if my feet were sliding at incredible speed. It was super high speed that I could not control myself. A cloud of dust was rising from the ground. And again my feet went faster and faster. Then my body started floating in the air: 10 cm, 20 cm.... and then UP! higher and higher, 5, 10, 20m, 50m......
I left the ground and I was dancing in the sky. After a while my dream melted away in the darkness of sleep. After several days I had the same dream. Once awake I felt confident that it was the same dream. Dream or reality, that time the stillness of a dream was definitely floating in the air.
But after several days I had the same dream. My steps were still accelerating, my body started floating and then flying at a high speed far from the ground. Afraid of this speed I screamed even though I understood I was only dreaming. The next day the same dream and the same scream again. «Am I dreaming?», «No, it's not a dream, I could really fly! This is not a dream anymore!». I dreamt of it for three days running. The last time I was convinced that it was not a dream but reality. I could fly up in the sky with my dancing feet. My dream is to perform that dream in real time and space. That means getting lighter than air by dancing. The body and time melted and merged completely in the air producing a new flow of life and making people believe that it is not a dream but reality.

All inclusive reality

My dream has to do with reality itself – but a different reality from the one we are so used to calling our own – not «knowing» anything else of that nature. Or so it seems to us.

As we know reality or «what is» – is the collection of phenomena that everyone agrees upon «is there». The outer – directly experienceable – existence. – Apart from that we also know that everyone has a private «inner-existence» space where however phenomena cannot be directly compared with other's. Thus it is considered of minor importance – but it is none the less there.

In my dream it is therefore of importance to realise that each of those private spaces really represent an opening into a real phenomenal existence complete with its own «physical» laws. No less important than the outer one.

Our present day science builds on the collection of data only from our outer existence – and not on wisdom/solutions directly received by us through our inner existence space. Therefore the total development of knowledge on this planet – supporting our present reality – is very one-sided. – It can be argued however that the latter way of understanding is the only one that makes «Science» a science.

This present day situation is responsible for the serious condition on our planet that we all recognize – even if it hurts to think about it. As one half of human-existence is completely kept outside reality. Consequently this set-up is robbing us of an existential freedom. And through it our minds are still being held in the grip of an «all knowing», but one-sided science-dogma. Thus preventing the development of our own potentials as beings bestowed with two connected existences.

My dream is therefore about mankind taking one step towards this new all inclusive reality: By founding a new enlarged branch of physics encompassing both of these human existences combined – a new Omniphysics – a tool for explanation in this new reality.

Einar Thorsteinn

Wolfgang Tillmans

A cure for Aids or even better a vaccine against HIV, so that the insane bond of love, sex and fear is forever broken.

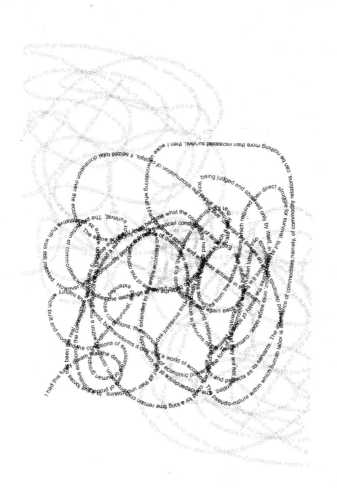

Rirkrit Tiravanija

Rosemarie Trockel

My great dream is to finish with dreams, but to believe
I am dreaming.

One does not choose one's dreams, as one does not choose one's poems, but if conditions can be set for the approximation of poems to dreams I propose that a hammock be hung on long cords between the farthest two points of the perimetrical walls of the new Foundation's building, while leaving a free space between them. The cords would be tense so that the weight of a human body on the hammock would make it nearly touch the ground.

Hopefully this installation will induce the state of torpor, indolence, laziness, that is the ecosystem of my dreams.

Tunga

I'm at my parent's home age 17, I lay down on the couch and fall asleep.

In my dream I see myself laying on the couch.

I get up and look outside the window that gives out to a little courtyard ending in a high brick wall of an adjoining apartment building.

In the middle of the courtyard three cats are floating as in a state of elevation, instead of hair they have short trimmed feathers that move frantically and are brightly coloured.

Without any interval, I then find myself sitting in a bus, the light is bright orange and the people in the bus look like aborigines their faces covered with red spots as from lovebites, their eyes closed.

I can physically feel the outside heat. Then it turns black and yellowish grinds of sand start falling from above until a pile of sand is formed.

LEVELS for a CAT

This dream happened last night. I am in the countryside, alone, except for my tiger-colored cat. I go to bed late, quite concerned because he has not come back home to sleep, as is his unchangeable habit. My sleep is deep and eventless until suddenly a dream begins. The scene is in my bedroom that is full of other people. In particular an old acquaintance, who is behaving in a most aggressive manner to the weaker persons present there. I feel ill at ease, and seek to protect a young child, whom I hug close to me. At that moment I have the intuition or sense that my cat has returned. I raise myself up through layers of dream and sleep, until I emerge from this side of lucidity. Almost in the same gesture of motion, I throw away my covers and look by the moonlight through the glass pane of the bedroom door. There he is, indeed, the cat standing up on his two hind legs, scratching the door to be let in, as is his habit. Half in the dream, and half in my body, with a sigh of relief, I get up, and open the door.

Outside the night is cool and full of spring smells. I wake up further only to realize there is no cat. The sight of him has disappeared into the thin air of the night. I go back to bed, fall asleep lightly. A few minutes later a scratch comes, and I see exactly the same scene of the mirage, with the animal at the door. This time I get up and let him in for real. I return to bed with the strong sense of having collapsed several levels of so-called reality.

Francisco J. Varela

Richard Wentworth

attention <u>H.U. OBRIST</u>
DEPARTMENT OF DREAMS
(LITERARY DIVISION)

I was making my way through a gigantic hall, four or more stories high. All manner of objects obstructed my route, but I knew that this was the way to the atom bomb. No sooner had I caught sight of the bomb, than a man moved purposefully toward it, accompanied by a young woman. I held back to see what they would do.

The man began to stroke the bomb, investigating all its characteristics, its smoothness and its flanges with the palms of his hands and the inquisitive tips of his fingers. While he was doing this, the young woman, his daughter perhaps, spoke gently to him. I was too far away to hear what she said.

It was then that I realised that the man was blind.

DREAM

Because of its insistence, one particular dream stays in my memory. In general, I can only remember the second one. In front of me I saw an enormous aqueduct on an island as wide as the aqueduct itself, made from large rock fragments which were crumbling and falling on the people (among the crowds, I also recognised my brother). The people were sitting in rows beneath the aqueduct and were unmoving, because they were dolls who were staring fixedly at the sky.

Mechanically, I turned towards the water and I went towards a bridge on which there were some skittles. A rival and I were each handling a bowling ball, and he threw his to start the game. This rival looked like Kogler. I did not know the result and I aimed at the skittles. When the ball hit the skittles and probably fell into the water, I changed into a ball, and then in the water I became a fish and I was caught with a hook from a crane on a motor boat. I think that it was the sort of boat used for shark fishing.

This was probably the most penetrating dream I have had in my life. It was in 1967.

Franz West

Dream 1

Banal Dream

I had just had a show at Goldsmith's College where Maureen Paley had said I had got off lightly with the bad space. I remember trying to look for Michael Landy and eventually found him deep in thought. We went to Carl Freedman's for dinner. This flat was just as I had imagined – Magnolia walls, small plain fire place.

Liza May Post was taping a box up with her designed clothes in. I asked her about the clothes and if they were completed. She looked at me a bit annoyed that Carl had told me about her making stuff in England. Anyway she still had the horns to put on.

Her hair was freshly cropped but no-one mentioned this and also a woman was helping her cook but was not introduced to us. Then I also made out that Maureen was there and beckoned me to talk to her. I thought it too rude to move over to her to whisper. Small shrills and screams were coming from Liza-obviously the food was not doing too good. I went over to Maureen and she disappeared behind a cardboard wall. I went over to see how the pud-dings were doing in the oven. The cooking came over and so did Liza.

Dream 2

Not banal dream

I was standing waiting for a tube train to come.
I noticed Jane and Louise Wilson on the platform,
they were in very high spirits. They were then on
the train tracks larking around. A train came in went
straight over them as they were standing up and
then reversed back in the tunnel.
Though completely crushed and obviously dying
they both managed to say it was what they wanted.

Ian Wilson

There was a discussion in New York City, on the 1st of November, 1998.

i have no dream

Cornel Windlin

High above the city amid the countless lights, affixed to the highest point of one of the tallest buildings, aircraft warning lights (C ing. Castaldi EO8 Segnalatori) transmit in morse code «Le Baphomet» a novel by Pierre Klossowski...

«Although he had always felt a profound aversion to the instrumental mode which here offered itself as a means to inform the expired breaths, he told himself that he had been wrong to dismiss its spiritual efficacy on the basis of the devices' appearance, to the point of never making use of them. For if these devices seemed too exclusively to favour the physical accidents of informable substance, nonetheless, this itself was but a purely analogical reminder created imperfect but perfectible; these elements, by virtue of their servile function, operated with all the more justice because he himself, a breath created and thus imperfect, could not rise to so sublime an impartiality as to dispense entirely with their service. Moreover, the instrumental mode was for the most part rectified by the presence of a sacred object which alone was fit to confer its emblematic character on the entire operation. Mechanically, these devices performed a ritual...

They argued thus with no end in sight until the bell pealed. "Be advised", said the radiant beauty, "that your condition will be worse here than down below, for no one will understand you!

They will interrogate you, for they also interrogate animals; they will torture you if you don't answer, for they also interpret the muteness of beasts; and they will make predictions from your cries and you will not be able to defend yourself! I shall lend you the voice of this child: it belongs to me and I myself move his tongue!"

"No, O generous soul! I do not wish to defend myself at all! For if I had to speak again, I should repeat shocking things which you would not dare to utter, were they even imputed to a mere anteater!"

"Go on, I shall faithfully translate your thoughts: charity knows not its own interests! But all that is condemned shall be made manifest, and all that is manifest light!"

"But he whose light is darkness, what darkness!" began to sneer the man who obstinately walked on all fours.

Then suddenly the anteater's form covered him completely again, and now only hissing these last words with its tensile, sticky tongue, it attacked the radiant figure and too slowly for Ogier's liking, lifted her veils: for her voluptuous splendours had already begun to appear when Ogier suddenly saw again his own cadaver twitch at the end of a rope and open wide his staring eyes; he cried out so loudly that he awoke with a start.»

DREAM-LESS

I am told not to dream of a free society because it is a creation by distant nations across the oceans. I am told not to dream of an independent press because it does not exist. I am told not to dream of the abolition of unjust laws because they exist to protect me.
I am told not to dream of a people free from racial divide because the time is not yet ripe. I am told not to dream because dreams are insidious attempts by external forces to infiltrate my mind and eventually destroy me. So I never dream. I chose instead the humid air of obedience, docility and unquestioning faith.

Dream of becoming a Chinese Doctor

I dreamed, twenty five years ago, of leaving my family, where all the members are doctors, for art.
I dreamed of becoming a real «black sheep», a rebel for freedom.
I dreamed of becoming an artist-traveller-observer for humanity.

I dream now of rejoining my family, of becoming one day a doctor in traditional Chinese medicine.
I dream of learning this «dialectic diagnosis», a creative process via «association of ideas and imaginations», a «figurative» evolution inside a chaotic area, not as concept or material but an authentic experience.
I dream of discovering the immune system as «second brain», and a concentrated attention on everyday experience as a healing.
I dream of healing myself by learning all that and of never forgetting to cure the patient as well as the disease.

Chen Zhen

...C'est ainsi que Michelet peut nous apparaitre comme un adepte de cette chimie a priori, de cette chimie fondée sur des rêveries inconscientes[15]. Pour lui, «l'eau de mer, méme la plus pure, prise au large, loin de tout mélange, est légèrment visqueuse ...Les analyses chimiques n'expliquent pas ce caractère. Il y a là une substance organique qu'elles n'atteignent qu'en la détruisant, lui ôtant ce qu'elle a de spécial, et la ramenant violemment aux éléments généraux». Il trouve alors sous sa plume, tout naturellement, le mot *mucus* pour achever cette rêverie mêlée où interviennent la vuscosité et la mucosité: «Qu'est-ce que le *mucus* de la mer? La viscosité que présente l'eau en général? N'est-ce pas l'élément universel de la vie?»

Parfois aussi la viscosité est la trace d'une fatigue onirique; elle empêche le rêve d'avncer. Nous vivons alors des rêves gluants dans un milieu visqueux. Le kaléidoscope du rêve est rempli d'objets ronds, d'objets lents. Ces rêves mous, si l'on pouvait les étudier systémetiquement; conduraient à la connaissance d'une imagination mésomorphe, c'est-àdire d'une imagination intérmediaire entre l'imagination formelle et l'imagination matérielle. Les objets du rêve mésomorphe ne prennent que difficilement leur forme, et puis ils la perdent, ils s'affaissent comme une pate. A l'objet gluant, mou, paresseux, phosphorescent parfois - et non pas lumineux - correspond, croynos-nous, la densité ontologique la plus forte de la vie onirique. Ces rêves qui sont des rêves de pate sont tour à tour une lutte ou une défaite pour créer, pour former, pour déformer, pour pétrir.

L'oeil lui-même, la vision pure, se fatigue des solides. Il veut rêver la déformation. Si la vue accepte vraiment la liberté du rêve, tout s'écoule dans une intuition vivante.

Extract from «L'eau et les rêves»

WITH RARE EXCEPTION, THE TEXT OF *SOGNI/DREAMS* REPRODUCES THE AUTHORS' ORIGINAL VERSION, WITH TOTAL RESPECT FOR THEIR STYLE.

Finito di stampare nel mese di maggio 1999
da Grafiche del Liri srl - Isola del Liri (FR)
per conto di Castelvecchi Arte c/o
Castelvecchi Editoria & Comunicazione srl